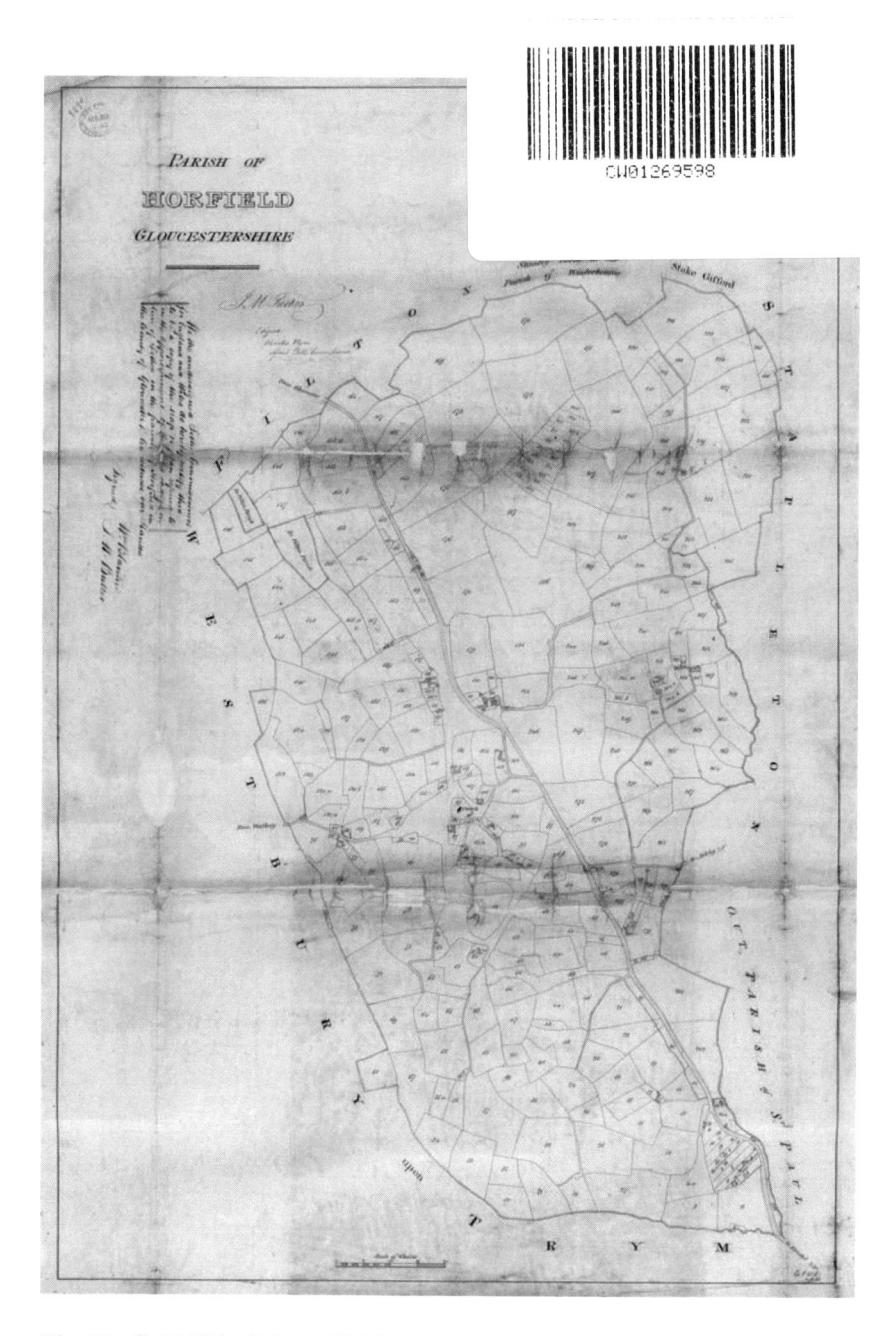

The Horfield Tithe Map – 1841

Acknowledgements

We would like to thank the following for their help with the publication of this book:

Bristol Record Office for permission to use the image of the Horfield tithe map and other documents; Linda Hall for permission to quote from her research on Downend House Farm; Bristol Record Office and Wiltshire and Swindon Record Office for access to records.

Denis Wright is especially owed a debt of thanks for his work reading and transcribing historic documents about Horfield, which have enabled us to go back beyond the 19th century.

Bishopston Horfield & Ashley Down Local History Society – *Publishers*

c/o Horfield Quaker Meeting, 300 Gloucester Road,
Horfield, Bristol, BS7 8PD

Published: 2007

Copyright: Authors and Bishopston, Horfield & Ashley Down LHS

ISBN-13: 978-0-9555826-0-8

All rights reserved. No part of this publication may be reproduced, stored in a retrieval system, or transmitted in any form or by any means, electronic, mechanical, photocopying, recording or otherwise, without the prior permission of the publishers.

Front Cover – extract from Benjamin Donne's "Map of the Country 11 miles round the City of Bristol", dated 1769. Courtesy of Bristol's City Museum and Art Gallery

Preface

The Horfield parish tithe survey, carried out in 1841, was part of a great national scheme for introducing a system of fair rents in place of out-moded tithe payments. Every plot of land in Horfield and every building (except for the most recent on Russell's Fields) was identified, surveyed, and valued and the results were published in 1843, together with a large-scale parish map. These bulky documents (EP/A/32/23) are kept at Bristol Record Office and the main object of this booklet is to help conserve the originals by making their content more readily available.

The value of the survey will be fairly obvious to anyone with an interest in parish history. It is the earliest known description of the entire ancient parish. It was published before any 19th-century partitioning for new parishes took place (St Andrew, St Michael and All Angels etc). A small amount of fieldwork will show that many features of the rural landscape displayed on the tithe map are still visible in suburban Horfield. The dimensions of Victorian housing estates were determined by medieval field boundaries and some tithe map buildings and sections of lane, field, and hedgerow still survive.

The text of the survey (with notes) appears in an appendix. A much reduced scan of the tithe map appears alongside a highlighted OS map of the parish for general reference. The sheer size of the tithe map means that when it is reduced to booklet form there are problems of legibility. To resolve this, the map has also been quartered and a short essay accompanies each of the four areas. The essays make no attempt to cover every aspect of an area. Instead, they concentrate on one main feature and are meant to illustrate the wealth of information contained in the survey as a whole.

The North-West section of the Tithe Map, showing the extent of Horfield Wood, since at least Medieval times. The wood is the grey shaded area at the boundary with Filton. The dark shading either side is due to a fold in the original map.

Horfield Wood   Denis Wright

Horfield wood is claimed to have been one remnant of a great forest which supposedly covered much of south Gloucestershire during the Middle Ages. Robinson, for example, thought that Horfield at the time of Domesday book, 'was either partly covered or surrounded by forests, which extended to the banks of the Severn',[1] and Frederick Jones hinted that much of the alleged forest still existed in more recent times, 'in the days of our great-grandfathers'.[2] Both writers confused Horfield with Horwood (near Wickwar)[3] and both seem to have been influenced by the Rev. Braine who contrived to place ancient Kingswood (east of Bristol) at the centre of a romantic greenwood, imagining a time, 'Seven centuries past [when] Kingswood, as a forest, was in its pristine beauty'.[4] Developments in archaeology [5] have altered this widespread Victorian view of the English landscape but the legend of a medieval forest surrounding Bristol keeps on surfacing. One recent (and curious) claim is that Bristol developed as a port because it was virtually inaccessible by road - 'Shut off from the rest of the country by hills and almost impassable forests'.[6]

The word 'forest' was a legal term introduced into England by the Normans to describe tracts of land appropriated by the Crown and governed by 'forest law'. There was no necessary connection with trees. So-called 'forests' might be heath, or moor, or fenland and their creation from c.1070 was a means of imposing authority over existing landowners by asserting a doctrine 'that all land ultimately belonged to the Crown'.[7] The Domesday survey reveals that only about 15% of England was wooded, roughly twice as much as in the late-19th century. The figure for woodland in Gloucestershire east of the Severn in 1086 was 9.6%.[8] This accords with William of Malmsbury's description of the vale of Gloucester, written about 50 years later, c.1140. It was a developed landscape, 'rich in corn and abundant in fruits [with] innumerable towns, excellent abbeys, and frequent villages', extending southwards as far as a 'very celebrated town by name Bristow'.[9] It is also clear from a Plantagenet Charter of 1228 relating to part of the Vale that disaforestation had nothing to do with a mass clearance of trees but was a relaxation of 'forest law'. The Charter allowed that, 'all men who have woods within the metes on this side of the Severn [ie from the Little Avon to the Bristol Avon and eastwards to the Cotswold escarpment] may now close, impark, and take, give, sell, or essart their woods', without reference to 'any forester or verderer or other minister of the king'.[10] In short, there was no medieval forest (as imagined by Braine and others) and nor had there been such forests (from the evidence of landscape archaeology)[11] for upwards of two millenia. William of Malmsbury's description of the Vale also shows that the real 12th-century 'Bristow' was not an isolated coastal enclave but a thriving regional trading centre, 'a resort of ships [from] beyond seas; lest a region so fortunate in native riches should be destitute of the commerce of foreign wealth'.

There was very little woodland in Horfield at the time of the parish tithe survey. It consisted of two small brakes or thickets (161, 226); three small plantations (88, 90, 278); a wood of 3 ½ acres called 'Horfield Wood' (165); and a wood of 14 acres called 'Huttom Wood', split into 18 parts (188-205). Total woodland in Horfield in 1841 thus amounted to 19 ½ acres, or 1.6% of the total acreage of the parish. Some of it was not ancient woodland. At least one of the plantations (90) was new since it stood on a section of highway abandoned during the 18th century.[12] The most peculiar item was Huttom wood. Traditionally, woodland belonged to a manorial lord. A wood might be leased out for a term of years, or local villeins might have customary rights to firebote, pannage, and the like, but the wood itself remained part of the lord's demesne. Huttom wood (or 'Hutton' as it usually appeared in manorial records)[13] was an exception in that it was not part of the demesne but was owned collectively by villeins (copyhold tenants), each farm holding one share. This arrangement, a probable replacement for customary rights in demesne woodland, can be traced to c.1550, to a reorganisation of land by the diocese of Bristol. Either Huttom wood belonged to the demesne before that date (though there was no reference to it), or (more likely) it was newly planted in the mid-16th century.[14] It may have been named after Robert Hutton, tenant of the largest copyhold farm at the Dissolution, the same farm also holding one of the brakes (226) at the tithe survey.

The most substantial piece of demesne woodland in Horfield in 1841 was the plot called 'Horfield wood' (165) which stood on the eastern side of the highway to Filton, and belonged to the Great Farm. There had once been more. According to Samuel Seyer's notebook (c.1814), Horfield wood 'which now is only on the Eastern side of the road, then was on both sides'.[15] His information came from parishioners. They also told him dubious tales of wicked deeds and of travellers fearing 'to pass that way in the evening'. Seyer was privately amused that Christian men should continue to spread such tales in enlightened times: 'The making of the Turnpike road contributed much toward letting in the light upon them: nevertheless *hodie manent vestigia ruris*' [traces of country ignorance still remain]. Bingham missed the joke and took the stories literally: 'I take this to mean that vagrants and footpads infested the neighbourhood'.[16] The story of a once larger demesne wood is, however, supported by the tithe survey.

Much English woodland was cleared by late-18th-century 'improvers' of land and this seems to have been true of Horfield. The death of Charles White, crushed by 'a loaded timber cart falling against [him]', reported in manorial records for 1811, may well have been part of that process. The probable dimensions of Horfield wood before clearance can be calculated from tithe survey plot-names. On the western side of the road in 1841, was a group of plots called Horfield Wood (150, 151a-b), all three recorded as arable in the survey. On the eastern side, one plot, Wood Leaze (167), had not been woodland even in the Middle Ages, as the name element 'leaze' suggests, but four other former woodland plots (163, 164, 166, 168) had been cleared mainly for arable by 1841, leaving only the Great Farm's wood (165) intact. From that evidence, a wood of over 40 acres had once straddled the highway at the boundary with Filton parish.

There had been other smaller woods. The Great Farm acquired its '3 acres of wood called Horfeilds wood' (165 above) c.1550, and at the same time '3 acres of wood called Balston grove' (possibly subsumed under 179 Rosemead & Grove in 1841) and 'a grove called the Marehay'.[17] Before the Dissolution, the Great Farm seems to have had more general access to demesne woodland, as suggested by an Abbey lease of 1532 which granted Thomas Walter 'All the wodds ffor there necessarye use'.[18]

That particular clause in the 1532 lease is an indication that woodland in Horfield, like woodland in parishes across the rest of England, was managed according to ancient practice.[19] It was a case of coppicing trees and using the regenerative capacity of many native species in order to grow wood to size. With minimal reworking and wastage, this 'underwood' was then used for a range of purposes, including domestic buildings, fencing, vehicles, and implements. Woodland was generally coppiced in rotation and contained only a scattering of mature timber trees.

Underwood remained more valuable than mature trees even in the 17th century. A lease on 'twoe acres & a halfe' of Horfield's demesne wood in 1663 described the plot first and foremost as 'underwood' and only secondly as 'woodground'.[20] It was bounded by other woodland strips and we know that it lay on the western side of the road because it 'abutteth on the highway on the south side and the land now or late in the tenure of William Dymock on the north side'. It was probably the plot called Horfield Wood (150) in the tithe survey. The lease called it part of 'Audleys wood' and contemporary records gave variant names (Harleys, Hareleaze, Hawdleyswood) for all woodland plots on that side of the highway. The managed state of the woodland is also clear from a manorial presentment of 1694 which named the same plot in Audleys wood as 'the Ridings', indicating that recent cropping had removed long swathes of underwood.

Manorial courts were mostly concerned that tenants of woodland kept their 'bounds' in good repair. These were often a ditch and bank topped by a fence and for Horfield wood the bounds included a leap gate (lypiate) across the highway, designed to let deer pass but not cattle or other livestock. A second leap gate stood at the northern entrance and was the responsibility of Horfield manorial tenants in Filton. Cattle were a particular problem for Huttom wood. It was entirely surrounded by fields belonging to the Great Farm and in 1779 a manor court noted that 'Huttam wood for want of the hedges being repaired is exposed to be much injured by young Cattle having free access thereunto'. The 'injury' to the wood was probably caused by cattle feeding off new growth. As Thomas Tusser had observed in 1557,

> When there is a fell of Underwood, the Buds that put out the Spring following, are exceeding juicy and tender...Oxen and Cows exceedingly delight to eat them, they will refuse the Grass, to crop them [21]

It seems likely that Huttom wood consisted largely of coppice stools - cut low to the ground. The whole wood was in fact described as coppice in 1852. [22]

By the mid-18th century, traditional usage of local woodland was in decline. When Duck Street gate needed replacing in 1753, the four tenants responsible for it turned to specialist wood-merchants and carpenters. They bought a new 'Oaken Gate' (12s) which came ready-made from Henbury (1s for haulage), together with 'Oaken Postes' (10s), and 'Oaken Quarters for Rails' (2d per foot). The oaken quarter was probably sawn because oak is hard to split. They also paid William Robson for the two days he spent erecting all this at 1s.6d per day.[23]

The medieval boundaries of Horfield wood were at least as old as the demesne fields around them. These were fields with early ploughland names, enclosed (according to Smyth) in the 13th century, [24] and later recorded at the Dissolution. [25] The names were preserved for the most part in the tithe survey - such names as le Breche, Longlond, and Northfeld (to the west of the highway), and Shutclose and Shurmore (to the east). A Temporality of 1428 (a term showing that the Horfield demesne was then leased out to laymen) gave the amounts of demesne arable and woodland. There were 100 acres of arable (*C acre terre arabilis*) and 20 acres of woodland (*xx acre bosci*).[26] These were clearly rounded estimates, and the quantities were not statute acres, but the proportion of arable to woodland (5:1) is likely to have been broadly accurate. The tithe survey revealed the ghost (mainly) of old demesne woodland, about 40-45 acres in extent, or 3.5% of the total area of the parish. Elsewhere in the demesne, which fields were cultivated or which lay fallow was likely to vary from year to year. In 1841, some demesne arable happened to be former woodland and some old ploughland (eg Great Mill Furlong, Five Acre Field, Great Breach) was pasture. In 1841, the proportion of arable (202 acres) to the ghost of Horfield wood was still roughly 5:1. This may be no more than coincidence but it does lend further support to tithe survey evidence for the medieval dimensions of the wood.

By the time of the Horfield tithe survey, the importance of local woodland had declined and much had already been cleared. However, local wood remained an important commodity in the case of Horfield Great Farm, the only surviving demesne farm. Tenants of the manor house were obliged to keep the late-medieval fabric of the building in good repair. In February 1841, the current tenant, Anthony Storey, wrote that the house had 'a great deal of wood in its construction' and, in spite of his best efforts, it was 'in a very dilapidated state'. Repairs to the house and to the estate in general meant 'that a very considerable fall [of wood] will be immediately indispensible'.[27] That obligation probably accounted for why one fragment (165) of Horfield Wood survived a little longer than the rest. The manor house was demolished in 1905.

A pollard Ash in the area of the former Huttom Wood: It is possible that this tree, one of several, may be a survivor from the wood itself, remnants of which are shown on maps up to c 1913 (see page 39).

References

1. W.J. Robinson, West Country Churches (Bristol, 1914), II, 52.
2. Frederick Jones, History of Bristol's Suburbs (reprint 1977), 31.
3. John Smyth, History of the Hundred of Berkeley, ed. Sir John Maclean (Bristol & Gloucestershire Arch. Soc., 1885) III. [Both writers were influenced by an error (re Horfield/Horwood) in Maclean's index rather than by Smyth's text].
4. A. Braine, History of Kingswood Forest (Centenary reprint, Kingswood History Society, 1991), 31.
5. W.G. Hoskins, The Making of the English Landscape (Penguin, 1985). [See the introduction for a brief summary of advances up to 1976]
6. Donald Jones, A History of Clifton (Phillimore, 1992), 4.
7. Oliver Rackham, Trees and Woodland in the British Landscape (Weidenfield & Nicholson, 1995), 165.
8. ibid., 48.
9. Samuel Seyer, Memoirs of Bristol and its Neighbourhood (Bristol, 1821-3), I, 446-7.
10. 12 Hen III c53.
11. Christopher Taylor, Village and Farmstead (George Philip, 1984), 47; Richard & Nina Muir, Fields (MacMillan, 1989), 122.

12. Denis Wright, The Wellington Hotel (alias The Ship) Horfield and a note on the line of the ancient highway through the parish from manorial records (Bristol & Avon Archaeology 19, 2004), 93-8.
13. Bristol RO, 32226 Box 22.
14. Denis Wright, Copyhold Farms in Horfield Parish (Bristol & Avon Archaeology) forthcoming.
15. Bristol RO, P/Hor/X/1a.
16. Fanshawe Bingham, Horfield Miscellanea (Portsmouth, 1906), 11.
17. Arthur Sabin, Some Manorial Accounts of St Augustine's Abbey, Bristol (Bristol Rec. Soc. 22, 1960), 178.
18. ibid., 175.
19. Rackham (1995), [see particularly 8 & 38].
20. Wiltshire RO, 1178/636.
21. Thomas Tusser, Five Hundred Points of Good Husbandry (Oxford, 1984), 275.
22. Ecclesiastical Commission of 1848 (House of Commons, 1852), Schedule 2.
23. Wiltshire RO, 1178/686.
24. Smyth, History of the Hundred of Berkeley, I, 114.
25. Public RO, SC6 Hen VIII 1240 m17/18d.
26. Sabin (1960), 173.
27. Ecclesiastical Commission of 1848, 84-5.

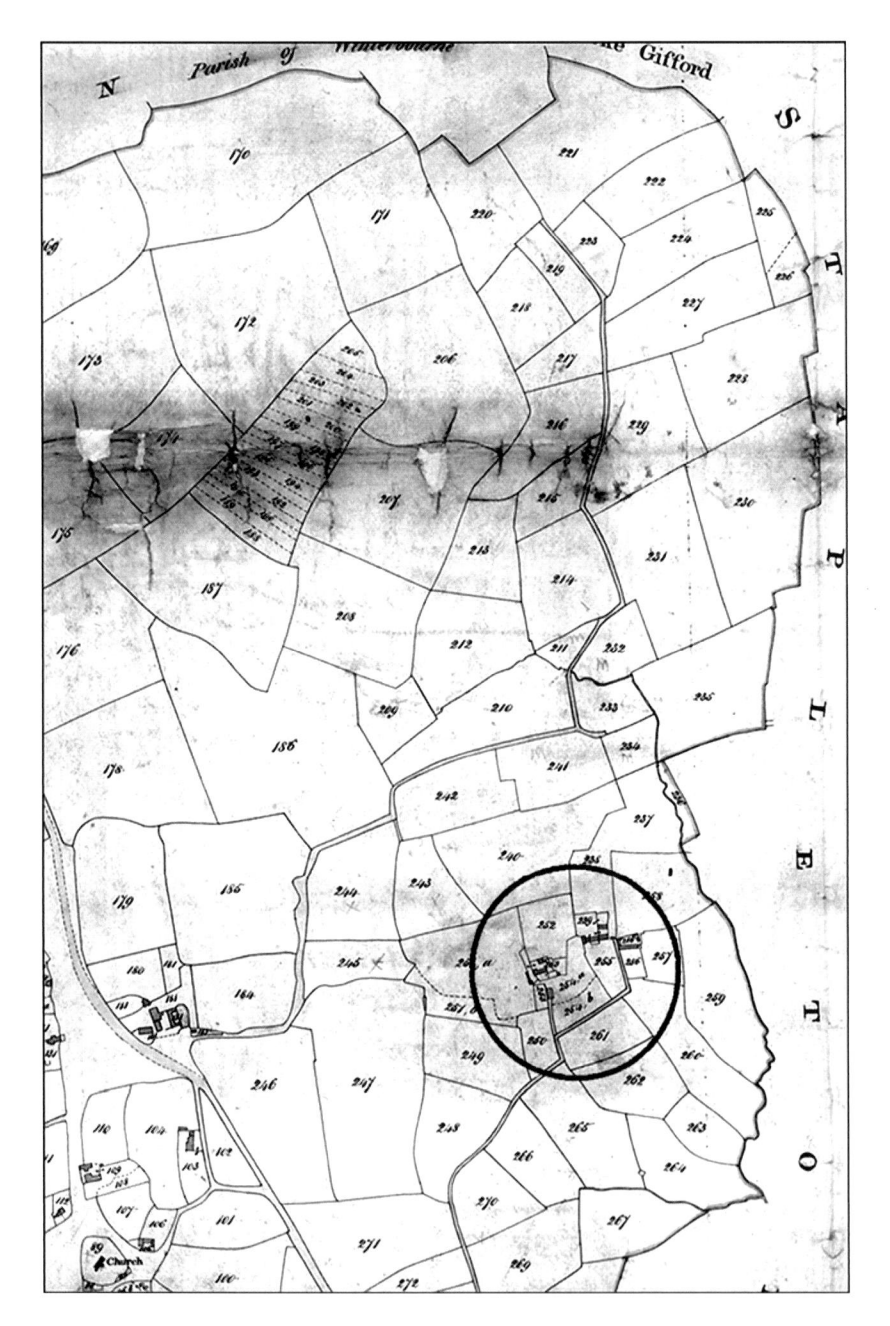

The North East section of the Tithe Map, the hamlet of Downend, is circled.

Downend   Andy Buchan

The north-east section of the parish is of interest for several reasons: it contains the remains of what may have been a small hamlet within the parish and it is still possible to see the medieval parish boundary and also some field boundaries.

Parts of the parish were bounded by a bank and ditch or hedge and ditch, but it is not clear if the whole parish was so enclosed or only certain sections of the boundary. An indication of the size of the ditch and accompanying hedge may be gained from a document dated 1829, which describes an agreement between William Townley of Stapleton parish and Edward Russell of the parish of Saint Paul[1], who owned a lease on Horse Hill (field 281) (See map on p30). The purpose of the agreement was to give William Townley access for properties he had in Stapleton parish to an "ancient public footpath" in Horfield parish which led to the turnpike road, (Gloucester Road). The agreement gave Townley permission to make a gap twelve feet wide (3.7 metres) in the hedge and to build a stone bridge over the ditch. The gap in the hedge was to be fitted with a gate. The document says that the bridge and gate must be maintained and also carefully defines who and what may use the new gate and bridge – foot passengers only, no horses, carts, carriages or mules. Interestingly it also says that it may only be used by inhabitants of the existing houses and not by people who may use any new houses that are built.

Evidence of a boundary ditch is still visible along the edge of the parish at field numbers 170, 221, 222, 225, 226, 228. The size of the ditch varies significantly being very shallow alongside fields, 222, 225, 226 and 228 and being wide and deep alongside 170 and 221. It is likely that this reflects places where the ditch has fallen out of use as a boundary and other places where it continues to be maintained. The ditch alongside fields 222, 225, 226 and 228 has narrow banks on either side: eroded sections show that they are made of blocks of the local White Lias limestone and clay. Hedges are present on the banks in some areas, but they look recent. The ditch alongside field 170 has a substantial bank surviving on the outer edge of the ditch and this is topped by a substantial hedge containing at least four or five species of tree, including Blackthorn, Common Hawthorn, Field Maple, English Elm and English Oak, suggesting at least an early post-medieval date for the hedge. Field 170 is maintained as a playing field directly up to the top of the ditch so it is not possible to say if originally the ditch may have had a bank on both sides. The ditch section alongside field 221 is slightly wider and shallower than the ditch alongside field 170. It appears to have banks on both sides, with substantial hedges growing on both of them, showing the same species listed above, suggesting at least an early post-medieval date. The current size and shape of the ditch are most probably due to its having fallen out of use as a boundary and no longer being maintained, in contrast to the section along field 170.

In the South Gloucestershire Sites and Monuments Record is a reference to a length of boundary bank/ditch being recorded behind the former Salvation Army Headquarters on Filton Avenue[2] – the record ascribes a medieval date to the structure. This section of boundary would be alongside field 169. No other information about the size, arrangement of bank and ditch or construction is given – no structures are visible at or above ground level. The field evidence supports the documentary record in showing that at least large parts of the parish boundary were delineated by a ditch, with a bank on at least its outer edge and in some cases on both edges. Observation on the boundary between the parishes of Filton and Westbury has also shown some evidence of a probable similar boundary ditch.

Probably of greater interest than the parish boundary are the remnants of what was very probably a hamlet within the parish of Horfield, called Downynge and later Downing, also Downs End in historical records of the 17th and 18th centuries and Downend since the middle of the 19th century. This was centred in the area around field 253 – at the lower end of Dovercourt Road.

At the time of the survey the hamlet consisted of three farms. No other houses are listed, although the 1841 and 1851 censuses show three further households. It is not known if all the families listed in the censuses were living in the known buildings or were living in less substantial buildings that have long since vanished. The 19th and 20th century details of who lived in the three known farms have been described in a booklet 'Downend, Horfield – A General History of the Forgotten Hamlet'[3]. Besides the farms no other information about the hamlet is currently known.

Two of the farms were leased by the same family since the mid-18th century, while the third was part of the Heath House estate. Of the three, two still remain. One, Downend Park Farm, at the end of October Lane, off Downend Road, is largely intact and represents the oldest surviving building in Horfield after the church. The second, Downend House Farm, on Dovercourt Road, exists partly as a façade and partly as a modern rebuild.

We know who the copyhold tenants were of all three farms since 1652[4]; but little is known of the history of the different sites, when the known houses were built, whether there were earlier buildings on the same sites and whether there were other houses. What is known is that there were farmsteads at Downend before the Dissolution and we know the names of four possible copyhold tenants. It is likely that the origin of the hamlet goes back centuries before the Dissolution.

Downend House Farm (256) belonged to Heath House from 1752. The house as it existed before the front third was knocked down and rebuilt, in the 1980s, showed many phases and several styles of building, different parts having had different uses over time. A side view essentially showed three buildings attached to each other, each of which had also been modified. An architect's floor plan also reveals that internally there were many different floor levels. It is likely that the original building was as old as Downend Park Farm, which is dated to the early 17th on stylistic grounds (see below).

What we do know from manor court records[4] is that in October 1764 "Joseph Whitchurch hath lately pulled down a messuage sometime since erected and built by one Edward Annely on a tenement and half yard of land". Edward Annely was the copyhold tenant of the property in 1734; it is known that the copyhold had passed to the Farmer family by 1740. What was meant by the phrase "pulled down" is not known: a comparison of the building as it was before it was rebuilt in the 1980s, see below, and a drawing of it on an estate map of 1767 for Heath House[5] shows a very similar building.

Downend House Farm - extract from Heath House Estate Map of 1767.

What is not known is whether Edward Annely built a new house or modified an existing building and similarly how much of the structure built by Edward Annely, Joseph Whitchurch "pulled down" before rebuilding. Clearly, he did not demolish the whole building in 1764, but probably re-built or remodelled part of it.

By the time the house was rebuilt in the 1980's, the central building had already been modernised to the extent that only one external feature that might be used to date it remained, namely a round-headed stair window at the back of the house, which dates to circa 1830-1840. The part of the building nearest to Dovercourt Road had sash windows with the frames flush with the outer face of the wall, suggesting an early 18th century date. This suggested date is further supported by the fact that one of the windows has 18 panes of glass, 9 over 9, which suggests a pre-1830 date for this part of the building.

Downend House Farm as it appeared in 1985, the upper picture shows part of the front of the house and the lower picture shows the back of the house.

Until the middle of the 18th century, the records show that Downend Park Farm, No 253 on the tithe map, and the other farm, No 239 on the tithe map, were held by different people. Successive members of the Webb family held Downend Park Farm, along with numerous other farming interests in and around Bristol and North Somerset, and Jonathan Newport held the other farm in the first part of the 18th century. In 1743 Ebenezer Hare obtained the copyhold of the land held by Jonathan Newport and in 1752 the Hare family also became the copyholders of the land formerly held by the Webb family. The Heath House Estate map shows all land immediately west of Downend House Farm as "Mrs Hare's land" which refers to Elizabeth Hare and Donne's map[6] of 1769 denotes a house in the vicinity as "Mr Ayres" (*sic*). Successive generations of the Hare family then held the farms until they were obtained by the City of Bristol early in the 20th century.

An early resident of Downing, whose family were possibly copyholders, was Agnes Edwards, widow of Robert Edwards, whose will was proven in 1628: in her will she leaves the contents of her house to her neighbour "Thomas Humfris" (*sic*). Unfortunately the will gives no details of exactly what goods and chattels she is leaving, so it is not possible to learn anything about her house from the will. The value of the contents is known from probate records to be £18 which is approximately equivalent to £2,500 today. We do not know at which of the three farms Agnes Edwards lived.

At the time of the tithe survey it appears that Henry Hare was running the two farms (copyholds) on customary lines. Both farms had all the usual indicators – a farmstead, a Home Mead, an orchard (or old orchard) and a piece of Hutton Wood. The tenant of Downend Park Farm, William Smith, held exactly 36½ acres within Hare's grand total of very nearly 90 acres; see plan A below and there is no reason to doubt that this was the actual arrangement on the ground.

However, the customary acreage for Downend Park Farm (known as Webb's at enfranchisement) was given as 49a 0r 29p: The clerk had made a small error of transposition – see his intended total below. It is clear from presentments in 17th century manorial records that some of the fields belonging to Webb's had once belonged to Hare's other farm Newport's and *vice versa*, see plan B below. In other words, what we see in 1841 is the result of some internal tidying up for the sake of convenience. Someone was always going to have to travel to the top of Lockly Lane but a comparison of the two plans shows that all the changes tried to make for greater tidiness for both farms.

Plan A showing fields belonging to Downend Park Farm at the time of the tithe survey.

Plan B showing fields customarily owned by Downend Park Farm and matching total at enfranchisement in 1852.

The tables below help illustrate the movement of some of the fields between the two properties:

A nucleus of property belonging to Downend Park Farm, common to both the tithe survey and the enfranchisement document

253	House & Homestead	0	3	10
252	Orchard	1	3	24
251a	Home Mead	5	2	39
251b	Remainder of Long Crate	1	1	36
250	Part of Long Crate	1	1	9
267	Part of West Close	4	1	14
264	Part of West Close	4	2	33

20

265	Part of West Close	5	1	4
248	Innocks	4	1	24
189	In Hutton Wood	0	3	8
Total		30	3	1

Bits of property added to Downend Park Farm from Newport's Farm by 1841 were

254a-b	Part of Old Orchard	2	0	7
262	Dunghill Close	3	2	32
Grand total		36	2	0

But Webb's customarily owned

241	Short Mead	4	1	9
235	Seven Acres	9	0	3
236	Part of Seven Acres	0	2	39
270	Little Axtons	3	1	8
255	Part of Old Orchard	0	3	35
Grand Total		49	0	15

At the time of the tithe survey, much of the land was pasture. An 18th century record[7] relating to the Webb family properties refers to a furnace, which may have been at Downing or may have been at another property within Horfield near Duck Lane: the exact location is not given and there is nothing shown on any known map. It is not clear if this was a smith's furnace or a small limekiln or similar. Small limekilns are known in several parts of the area and it has been suggested that these may have been to treat limestone, so that it might be used to improve pasturage and other agricultural improvements[8].

Of the two farmhouses themselves, about one, Downend Park Farm we know a great deal, of the other we know nothing. We know that it was called Newports, but apart from this, there are no drawings, paintings or photographs or other records of it, which might enable an estimate to be made of its age or its development.

Downend Park Farm is considered, on stylistic grounds (style of building, internal fittings, comparison with similar buildings of known age) to have been built c 1630[9]. It was then extended in the 18th century and re-roofed probably in the 19th century. Unlike Downend House Farm, there is no evidence at least on the exterior that the property was significantly changed to reflect later styles of windows or doors. However, within the house there is evidence that some changes were made at various times within the 17th and 18th centuries – addition of fireplace surrounds, wall panelling etc. In spite of this the house still retains some of the original iron window catches etc.

It is built of the local white Lias limestone and is two and a half storeys high with a pantile roof; the front door opens onto a small lobby, behind which is a narrow dairy. To one side is the hall or kitchen and to the other side is the parlour, each with a fireplace in the end wall. When it was built it would have been considered a good quality house. This is based on various architectural details including the regular stonework, the chamfered and stopped overlintels and the use of king mullions. The stair goes all the way up to the attic and it has been suggested that this fact and other evidence within the house suggests that originally the attic area was divided into three rooms, probably lit by dormer windows. The extension on the eastern-end of the house was probably added in the mid 18th century. It is possible that the outbuilding to the east of the house is contemporary with the house. The house is well known because of two fireplaces glazed with Bristol blue and white Delft tiles, which were in the house.

This shows the front of the house before its recent restoration. Most pictures of the house back to the late 19th/early 20th century show the front of the house partly hidden by plants or ivy.

The rear of the house as it appeared c 1980 before restoration when some of the outbuildings were still present.

References:

1. Bristol Record Office, 35447, Box 8, bundle LX11
2. South Gloucestershire SMR, ref. 14012-SG8130
3. Baker, J., Downend, Horfield – A General History of the Forgotten Hamlet, 1992. (Bristol Record Office, 40457/1)
4. Denis Wright, pers. comm.
5. Bristol Record Office, AC/PL/88
6. Benjamin Donne, "Map of the Country 11 miles round the City of Bristol", 1769, Bristol City Museum and Art Gallery
7. Wiltshire and Swindon Record Office, 1178/660
8. Robin Styles, pers. comm.
9. Linda Hall, pers. comm.

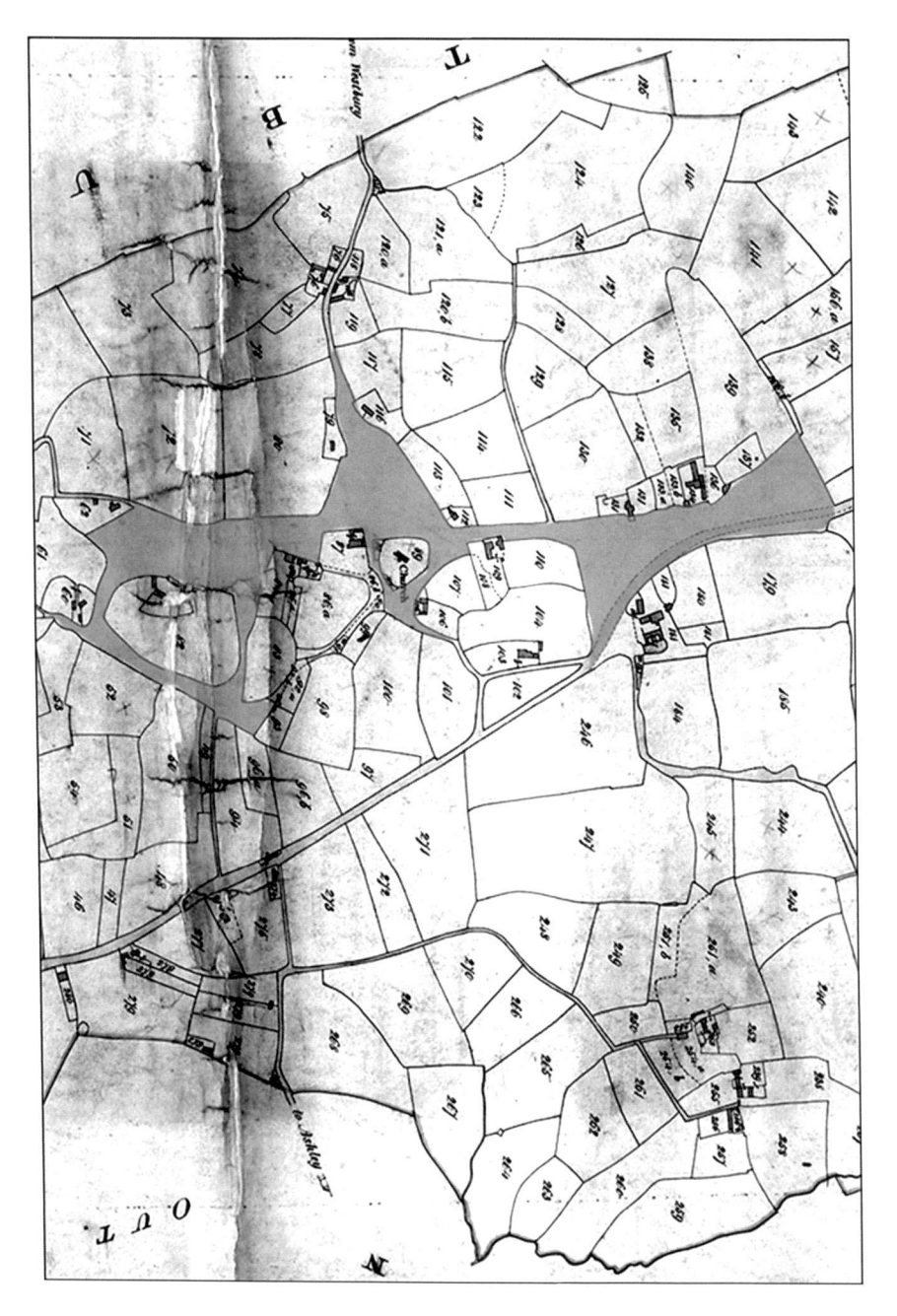

The central section of the Tithe Map, showing the common and the centre of the parish. The common is shaded grey.

Horfield Common   Denis Wright

The common is probably the single most striking and enduring legacy of Horfield's ancient past. There are few obvious and visible signs of a medieval township which once occupied the area of the common, except for items like the west tower of the parish church, but the tithe survey and other documents give much information and the common itself provides a living context. In this way, we can identify sites of medieval farmsteads and a manor house, or trace the line of medieval roads through the settlement. This in turn raises speculation that Horfield church may occupy a sacred pagan hilltop site, by a spring, where at one time three ways met.[1]

At the tithe survey, Horfield common was owned by John Shadwell as part of his lease on Horfield manor from bishops of Bristol. Shadwell was last in a line of manorial lessees (*firmarii*, so-called Lord Farmers) dating back to the dissolution of St Augustines Abbey. Shadwell's death in 1849 brought an end to the manorial system in Horfield, his leasehold property reverting to the current bishop, James Henry Monk. Monk was legally entitled to a considerable personal fortune but, in 1852, he donated most of his landed interest in the parish (including the common) to a newly founded Horfield Trust, which was designed to provide a regular income for the diocese through a mixture of housing development and agriculture. The Trustees eventually sold Horfield common to Bristol city council on October 4 1908 for £400.[2] This represented roughly one fifth of its value as grazing recorded 70 years earlier at the time of the building of the parish school.

The present common is not quite the same common as shown in the tithe survey. The making of Kellaway Avenue after the 1914-18 war diminished it and, perhaps by way of compensation, part of a field (80 Great and Little Hughes) was turned into common, the former extent of the old field boundary marked by a solitary oak. The city council also acquired Ardagh ('formerly known or called by the name of the Poplar Cottage') together with its 5 ½ acre Home Mead (81-2), for £4,850 from Wiclif Warner on March 31 1921.[3] A piece of Ardagh's Home Mead (marked by a curving boundary of limes) was similarly converted into common.

There had been other small changes to the common shortly before the tithe survey. Samuel Seyer spent much of his incumbency (1813-26) corresponding with tenants, lessees, and lawyers to get agreement on the purchase of an acre of common for a parsonage (87), completed in 1825.[4]

His successor, Henry Richards (1828-64), had no such trouble acquiring in 1838 a smaller piece of common (28 perches, value £14) for a school next to the churchyard,[5] supported as it was by an Act of 1836 which found it 'expedient to promote the Education of poor Children in the Principles of true Religion and useful Knowledge'.[6] There had also been earlier 'encroachments' reported in manorial records.[7] William Thomas 'Erected a Cottage in a lane from the Church' (91) in 1804 and William Matthews tried to secure the property in 1809 by enclosing 'part of the Common leading to a lane commonly called Abigail lane'. Tenants of Hughes's (79) had also encroached on the common 'in a course of years', gradually extending a hedge to 'fourteen lugs in length and one lug in breadth [ie 231 ft x 16 ½ ft] from the Ancient hedge' (1795). There is no record of encroachment before that date, so, with those exceptions, the boundaries of the common shown at the tithe survey are likely to have been late-medieval.

Arguably the most important change affecting the common in modern times occurred in the early-18th century. It was caused by the Bristol Roads Act of 1727 [8] which led to a straightening and general improvement of the parish highway. The common lost no land but an evident increase in traffic changed its customary usage. A manor court of 1741 recorded that the common gates were no longer kept habitually shut but 'frequently lie open a considerable Time together' and there seemed to be no solution except 'a Fence to enclose the Common from the Gloucester Road'. Within a few years, gates at the entrances to the common had been dispensed with altogether. Those across the turnpike road probably went first, followed by the Duck Street gate, 'a thing not being thought necessary' (1774), across the road to Westbury. Later efforts to conserve the common had as much to do with tidiness as ancient function. Courts objected, for instance, to tenants keeping dunghills on the common (1763, 1801), or stacks of tree trunks (1763, 1810), or removing 'greensward' (1812), or failing to drive on the roads. A presentment of 1808 recorded that,

> many persons have been in the Habit of driving Carts Waggons and other Carriages over the common instead of the Roads whereby the Turf and Commonage have been much destroyed to the great Injury of the Commons. The Jury therefore recommend that Boards with Notices inscribed thereon be placed at the entrances of the common in the following places viz. One on the North East entrance from the Gloucester Road [Dorian Road]; one other at the entrance of the Ship Lane opposite Mr Narroway's Gate [top of Wellington Crescent]; and a third at the

entrance on the West side of the said common [bottom of Wellington Hill West] forbidding all Persons with Waggons Carts and other Carriages from driving off the Bye Roads which are provided and repaired at the expense of the Parish

Traffic may have been destroying the 'Turf and Commonage' but it is also clear from references to dunghills etc that some tenants no longer valued common pasturage in quite the same way as their ancestors.

For centuries, the common had provided valuable additional grazing. It was grazed for 9 months of the year but was closed ('hained') annually from the feast of the Purification (February 2nd) until May 3rd to let the grass recover. The number of grazing animals was restricted, each farm entitled to its 'stint'. Any animal exceeding the stint was treated as a 'strayer', locked in the common pound, and released only on payment of a fine. A hayward (*agrophylar*) was appointed annually from amongst the tenants by rotation in order to enforce the system. These and other features date from 17th-century manorial records but the system itself was probably ancient. It was certainly operating in the late-Middle Ages, as shown by a 1532 lease on the Great Farm which entitled Thomas Walter to half the price of any 'strayars' lawfully pounded.[9] Reponsibility for the fabric of the pound, situated next to the Great Farm (181), had passed to manorial lessees at the Dissolution. A presentment of 1655 noted that the pound was 'out of repayre' and routinely expected the current lessee, Mrs Elizabeth Jackson, to repair it. All other 17th-century boundaries about the common were the responsibility of individual tenants, or, in the case of lane gates and the churchyard, their collective responsibility.

Presentments regarding the common in the 17th century tended to be brief, suggesting that an ancient unwritten code was still widely accepted and understood. They served mostly as reminders to 'all the Inhabitants of the Parish' to check their boundaries before the next open season, sometimes naming a key date, 'before the third day of May next', and always stating the fine for non-compliance, 'on paine of iijs.iiijd every one makeing default' (1653). Amongst the few recorded exceptions to those routine presentments was an instance of pound breach. In 1694, Mary Hughes widow impounded some beasts belonging to James Alleyn 'for trespassing in her ground'. To make matters worse, they were 'cother Beasts' (ie suffering from anthrax). James Alleyn then 'did break the pound & took out his Beasts without the consent of this sd. Mary Hughes & wee do fine him for the offence 3s.4d'. A distinction was drawn between 'Beasts' and other grazing animals. The term may have meant fatting cattle (specifically bulls), or possibly oxen, but, whatever they were, they had a will of their own and needed to be restrained. In 1700, all tenants were required to depasture their animals until 'the Beasts were tayed up', and in 1701 John Adlam was fined for failing to do this.

Presentments became more explicit as the manorial system itself fell into decline during the 18th century. The customary dates for haining issued in October 1735 were followed by an explanation that 'no Tenants shall presume to fold any Cattle on the said Common during the time appointed', as though some tenants were unfamiliar with the practice. Rules regarding number and type of animal permitted during the grazing season were also made explicit for the first time in the same year.

> every Copyholder or Customary Tenant shall depasture & fold upon the Common field one Horse, Beast or for want of that two Cows or three yearlings Beasts & no more in any one year as the Stint of Common in respect of their respective tenement

There is no means of telling whether the court was imposing an accepted customary limit or a new one, or indeed whether it had always been customary to change the stint from one year to the next, depending on the market, or other variables. Given the number of farms in the parish, up to 54 yearling beasts may have been grazing the common in the summer of 1736. A manor court of 1774 set fines for the release of impounded animals at '3d per head for all horses and cattle & for sheep one farthing per head', indicating that one horse was likely to eat the same amount as 12 sheep. In that case, there may have been up to 216 sheep grazing the common. In 1769, 'every Person putting Beasts on the Common' was required to 'mark the same with the initial letters of his Name'. There is no means of telling whether that practice also was customary, or a recent innovation.

There was some parish rivalry over commonage. Filton geese were banned from Horfield common (even in 'Coopes') in 1660, 1667, and 1676 and Horfield geese were banned from Filton common in 1677 and 1678. The geese (probably in all 5 cases) belonged to a Filton resident, Thomas Wade, who happened to be a copyholder within Horfield manor and the whole issue may have arisen because the creatures were a nuisance in any public place. Pigs were tolerated on Horfield common (1700) so long as they had rings in their noses but unringed they posed a serious threat to the commonage. Both geese and pigs were banned altogether in 1835.

Rights of common were held by copyhold tenants, successors to the villeins of Domesday Book. Copyhold farms were usually named after their tenants (or former tenants) and the following list gives the names current at the time of manorial enfranchisement in 1852.[10] The majority (fourteen) of the farmsteads were clustered around the common itself (from the north anti-clockwise):

131 Andrews'; 112 Thomas's; 116 Combes' Parcel; 118 Usher's;
76 Codrington's; 79 Hughes'; 62 Merefield; 60 The Quab;
81 Dymock's; 84 Attwood's; 92a Townsend's; 105 Quarrington's;
109 Bennett's; 103 The Ship

There were also three copyhold farmsteads at Horfield Downend:
253 Webb's; 239 Newport's; 256 Farmer's

Another farmstead, 17 Jefferies', lay 1 mile south of the church. Of the exceptions to common naming practice, The Ship was the village alehouse and two adjacent properties, Merefield and The Quab, were named after boggy ground at the source of Horfield brook. Farmsteads were extended or rebuilt over the course of centuries. Some were gentrified, or, like The Ship, put to special use, but all, with the probable exception of Merefield, occupied medieval sites.

References

1. Richard Morris, Churches in the Landscape (Phoenix, 1997). See a discussion of paganism in 'A Voice from the Well', 57ff.
2. Bristol City Council Archives, 06807.
3. Ibid, 07085.
4. Bristol RO, See Seyer's parish notebook (P/Hor/X/1a) and a draft letter to the Reverend Hare (P/Hor/1/10v).
5. Ibid, P/Hor/Sch/2a.
6. Act, 6-7 Will IV c70.
7. Bristol RO, 32226 Box 22.
8. Act, 13 Geo I c12.
9. Arthur Sabin, Some Manorial Accounts of St Augustines Abbey, Bristol (Bristol Rec Soc 22, 1960), 175.
10. Ecclesiastical Commission of 1848 (House of Commons, 1852), Schedule 1.

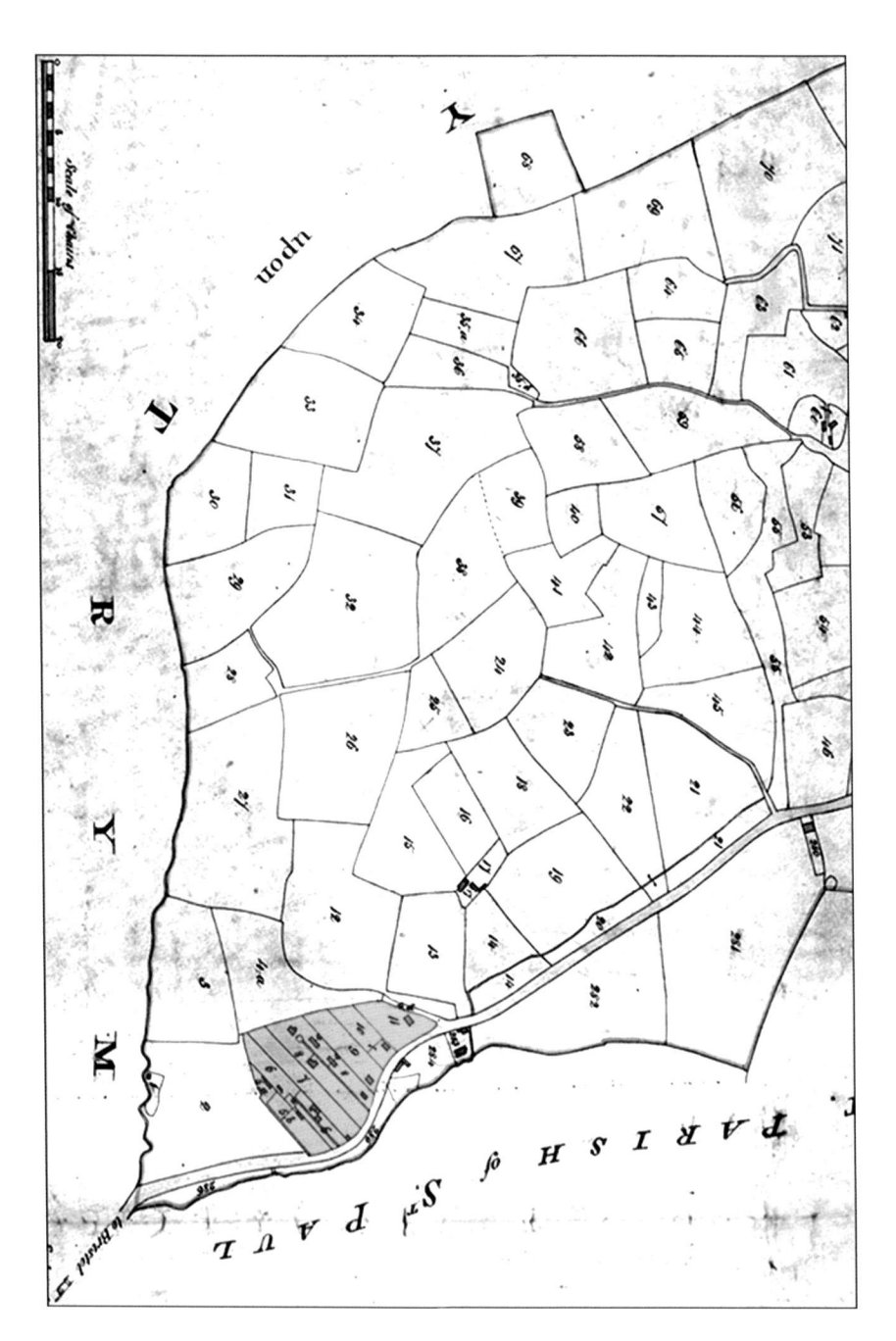

Southern section of the Tithe Map showing Neylor's Cottages, shaded grey.

Neylor's Cottages   John Hyde

This chapter deals with the beginnings of modern development in Horfield during the early 19th century and particularly with a place called Neylor's Cottages in the south of the ancient parish. The tithe map showed 22 dwellings occupying 7 strips of land (tithe numbers 5-11) lying on the west side of Gloucester Road. In today's terms, it was an area stretching from Meridian Terrace up to the Bristol North swimming baths. The whole area was known as Neylor's Cottages probably because Henry Neylor was the most active developer, leasing more of the available strips than anyone else and building 14 of the houses. The development dated from 1823 and was part of a gradual expansion of Bristol during the Industrial Revolution. Six other nearby houses are shown on the tithe map and were probably built during the same decade. Five of them stood on the opposite side of the highway in small paddocks (283-4) backing onto Horfield brook (between Bolton Road and the alleyway next to Peacock's) and the sixth was Conyger Dell cottage (1) standing by Cutlers Mills Brook. The only other nearby building shown on the tithe map was the farmstead known as Popes or Musty's farm (17), which was much older than the Neylor's development. The building of Neylor's Cottages also coincided with improvement of Bristol's turnpike roads, culminating (in the case of Horfield) in a new section of highway (Cheltenham Road), completed in 1824. These improvements were mainly due to the appointment in 1815 of John MacAdam as surveyor for Bristol roads.

Neylor's Cottages occupied the eastern end of a field called Broadway, the part nearest the highway, leaving the rest of the field (4a) as undeveloped pasture accessed from the highway by a lane (4b). The site was convenient because it was only half a mile from Stokes Croft (Bristol's northern boundary in medieval times). It may also have been selected because it contained an old quarry and there was possibly ready access to building stone.

There is no doubt that stone had been quarried in the area for many years. It is already described as "an old quarry" in an agreement dating from 1713 which is looked at in detail below. Although the exact whereabouts of the quarry are uncertain, there is evidence in another document of the 1850's, that stone could be excavated from field strips 7, 8 and 9, but perhaps quarrying took place over the whole area.

In any event, the first definite reference to the quarry is detailed in an agreement dated the 3rd of July 1713[1] The agreement was between "Obadiah Webb of Westbury Sup[er] Tryme in ye county of Glou[ceste]r Gent of the one p[ar]t" who was copyhold tenant of Broadway field "and John Bruton, of the out p[ar]ish of St. James in ye said County of Glou[ceste]r, yeoman, John Hobbs Jun[ior] of ye same p[ar]ish Yeoman & John Wood of ye City of Bristol, scavenger of the other parts". This allowed the three Johns to enter "an old Quarry of Stones lying & being in a certaine Close called Broadway situate near the said City of Bristol but within ye parish of Horvell" in order to "dig take and carry away w[i]th Carts and Carriages such stones as they cause to be raised". The document is extremely convoluted, lacks punctuation and is open to interpretation, but it is reasonably clear that the length of the agreement was for three years, albeit subject to reverting back to Obadiah Webb for one day at the end of each 12 month period. Perhaps this was to avoid any question of squatters' rights.

The financial arrangements are much less clear, revolving as they do around "Sixty horse cart Loads of [not more than] Tun weight of Stone each Cart to be drawne with fower horses". It appears that the target for Obadiah was not only to guarantee him a minimum return, but also to restrict the amount of stone the men removed! He charged them 4d[2]. (old money) for each ton load taken which means that 60 loads made him "at most the Sume of Twenty shillings of lawfull money of great Brittain". Each year, the men "soe shall continue on in every year to pay for every sixty loads soe digged" until "ye Sume of Twenty pounds" is reached thus giving Obadiah sixty pounds over the three year period. This amount was also guaranteed if the men "shall neglect or fayle to work in ye sd Quarr & thereby raise & carry from hence noe stones att all then nevertheless they ye sd John Bruton [etc] shall yearly pay & satisfie unto the said Obadiah Webb the Sume of Twenty Pounds until Sixty Pounds is raised & payd". There is no indication of how Obadiah kept a check on how much stone was removed by the men. Perhaps a tallyman or agent was employed.

The agreement was not totally loaded in Obadiah's favour. There was an item included that discharged the men from their responsibilities if Obadiah "obstructed or hindered in working & raiseing Stones in ye said Quarry". However, Obadiah also reserved the right "for his owne use & none other…to raise some loads of Stones in ye said Quarry" and "it shall be lawful for him…so to doe"!

Exactly what use was being made of the stone is open to debate. There is evidence in the 1841 census that a lime kiln was in operation close to the Neylor's cottages area (just across Horfield brook in what was to become Saint Andrew's parish) and the kiln could well have been working one hundred years before at the time of the agreement. The geological map for Bristol shows the locality to be mainly clay with bands of limestone so that would make the stone suitable for that purpose. However, a 19th century document shows that the stone was also suitable for building, so perhaps it was used for both. The fact that Obadiah reserved the right to take stone for himself suggests that at least some of it was building stone, although it is also possible that he had an interest in operating the kiln himself or in partnership with someone else.

There was a memorandum added to the agreement in November 1733 that, "John Underwood of the P[ar]ish of St James in ye Citty of Bristol scavenger" had taken from Obadiah Webb (who by this time had moved to Long Ashton) "a piece of ground…lying in the Parish of Horfield…called or known by the name of Broadway in wh[ich] there is a Quarry of Stones for the Term of Twenty one years …at the yearly Rent of Four Pound of lawfull Brittish money to be paid Quarterly". Obadiah reserved the right to "have liberty (if he thinks fitt) to dig or work the same, paying…to the said John Underwood reasonable damages". The reasonable damages are not specified! John himself was at "liberty to plow the said ground for two or three Crops" but he must give it "a good & sufficient Coat of Soil upon his laying of it down the last Crop" and to "keep & leave the Bounds belonging to said Ground in good repair & not to pound onto said Ground, but to leave it in Husbandlike manner when his Term is expired". John Underwood's occupation was that of scavenger which entailed cleaning and removing the refuse from the streets. Now it is quite likely that the refuse found in the Bristol streets of the 1730's, would have contained a fair proportion of what may be delicately termed "night soil". Did he have ready access to the material required to give "a good and sufficient Coat of Soil" when laying down his last crop?

The next significant date in the development of the locality is 1822, when an outline of a private Act of Parliament[3] was drafted. This enabled "the Bishop of Bristol [the owner of the land]…to grant building leases on an Estate in Horfield" and steered the way to the building of Neylor's cottages. At this time you needed a private Act to build on farmland or to alter roads etc. in fact, an early form of planning permission. There is no trace of the Act in the records held in the House of Lords, which is not unusual.

The estate in question was supposed to be part of a leasehold estate called "Lamb's", which according to the Act was leased by the Bishop to "Geo Lampriere Esq in trust for Dr Shadwell and others". In fact, the houses were built on part of the copyhold field called Broadway which was leased to Dr. Shadwell. "Lamb's" had been used merely as a cover to avoid legal complications and to ease the passing of the Act!

In any event, the Act went on to specify that, "it shall be lawful for the...Lessees of the said Estate to contract with any...persons whomsoever to let to him or them any part or parcel of the said Estate for the Term of 80 years for the purpose of building upon and Improving, at the greatest annual reserved rent that can be reasonably gotten for the same". It was likely that more cash would be generated from houses than from agricultural use, so people were encouraged to build more on the "part or parcel" that was let to them. However, the terms of the Act were a lot less grasping than most of today's developers as there was a proviso that "no Houses or Buildings of any description shall...be erected on any part of the said Ground within fifty feet of any other House or Buildings and that not more than one Acre of Ground shall be granted in any one lease and that there shall be at least ½ an Acre allotted to each House as a pleasure Ground or Garden" and "that no manufactory or noxious business be carried on there"!

Thus it was, that the earliest suburban development in Horfield referred to in the opening paragraph, came about. We have no real idea what the houses looked like as nothing survives to the present, but if the ground plans shown on the tithe map are accurate then some of them do look to be of reasonable proportions. The ground plans also show that the clause regarding the 50 foot distance between houses had largely been adhered to. We can be reasonably sure they were stone built, as the Shadwell estate documents[4] which record the ownership of the land from the 1830's to the 1880's, show that on April the 9th 1858 an indenture for a term of 60 years, from H.E. and J.E.T. Shadwell, was issued to "Richard Abbott plumber of Bristol" (who had taken over Neylor's lease of plots 7, 8 and 9). This indenture indicates that Richard was "at liberty...from and out of the said premises or any part thereof to raise and get stone to be used in reinstating, rebuilding or repairing the messuages and other buildings...or in the erection of other messuages or buildings on the said premises but for no other purpose".

Thanks to the census of 1841 and 1851 we can name and identify some of the properties marked on the map. The dwelling in tithe number one for example, changed its name on a regular basis. In the tithe survey of 1841 it was called "Conyger Dell Cottage" but in the census of the same year it is picturesquely named "Horfield Cottage in the Wood". By 1851 it is described in the introduction to the census as the "Turnpike Gate Cottage in Dewgards Wood" and in the body of the census two properties are noted, "Dewgards Wood Dell Cottage" and "Dewgards Wood Cottage"! Perhaps these are the enumerator's descriptions rather than the actual names. Cottages were often known by different names by different people. It was common for local people to refer to a dwelling by the occupant's name, particularly if they had lived there for some time. Other buildings identified on the map are the Horfield Inn (11), Beehive cottage (6), Prospect House (5b) and Horfield Villa (5a). The inn was not the pub of that name now called the Bristol Flyer, the original building was located away from the road and was taken down and rebuilt on the site of the present pub presumably to be closer to the highway.

The 1851 census shows that the Neylor's cottages estate was still thriving and had in fact grown. Perhaps the most surprising difference to the 1841 census is that apart from two families, the Hayter's who lived in Sydney cottage and Mary Panes of Horfield Villa, all the original residents had moved on. Mary was described as a "landed proprietor" and was probably running a boarding house as there were five other people in the house at the time of each count, but only Mary was in both. Several buildings had disappeared (or changed their names), but to make up for this, 14 new ones had appeared.

Probably the major development of the intervening ten years was the building by 1851 of upmarket villas alongside the main road, just to the south of Neylor's cottages. They are still standing today and line that part of the Gloucester Road now called the Promenade. Despite the fact that their frontages are now shops, wine bars or business premises, a glance above these establishments confirms what handsome houses they must have been. There is also a terrace of 4 houses on the right hand side of the small hill (now Claremont Road) which is off the northern end of the Promenade, which is part of the same development. Despite attempts over the years to "modernise" the terrace, they still retain a lot of original features and one can get a good impression of how they would have looked in their heyday. In

1851, The Promenade was called Elton Terrace and Claremont Road was Claremont Crescent.

The families who moved into these houses were affluent and well-to-do compared to their neighbours on the Neylor's development. Apart from a clergyman, Thomas Hething, who lived on his own at 17 Elton Terrace, there was at least one servant in all the houses and several had two. The difference was also reflected in the occupations of the two communities. The newcomers tended to own their own business or to be members of professions whereas the Neylor's occupants were mainly working people.

The next significant evidence for change in the general layout of the area is highlighted in Lavar's map of Bristol and Suburbs (see below). The map is undated but was probably produced in 1877. We can say this as the Wesleyan Chapel in Redland Road, which opened in 1878 is not shown, but two companies Dunscombe the optician and Tucker the chemist, who both advertised on the back of the map, were founded in 1876 and 1877 respectively.

The map shows Berkeley and Egerton Roads are in place and built upon. Elton Terrace (the Promenade) is marked and the terrace of 4 houses in Claremont Crescent (Claremont Road) is also evident, but not clearly. However, they must have been in place as they were in the 1851 census and are there today. Shadwell and Tyne Roads had been laid down but there is no sign of any housing being built on them. The field strips of the Neylor's estate are still shown, but fewer buildings are drawn in. Only 7 as opposed to 22 when the estate was built in the 1820's. This was obviously the beginning of the end for Horfield's first suburban development. The O.S. map of 1881 showed a complete redevelopment had occurred and all the cottages had been swept away. The road layout we are familiar with today had been established and built upon.

What paved the way for the collapse of Neylor's cottages? Perhaps the answer lies in a paragraph of the 1822 outline Act which says "That when the said term of 80 years is expired within 26 years it shall be lawful to…Surrender up the Messuage Land or premises to the said Lord Bishop". If 26 is taken from 80, that gives us 54 years, if the contracts date from 1822 then by 1876 the contract could be terminated. It may be that all concerned realised it was in their best interests to take down Neylor's cottages with their generous quota of land and redevelop with the more densely packed housing which we have now.

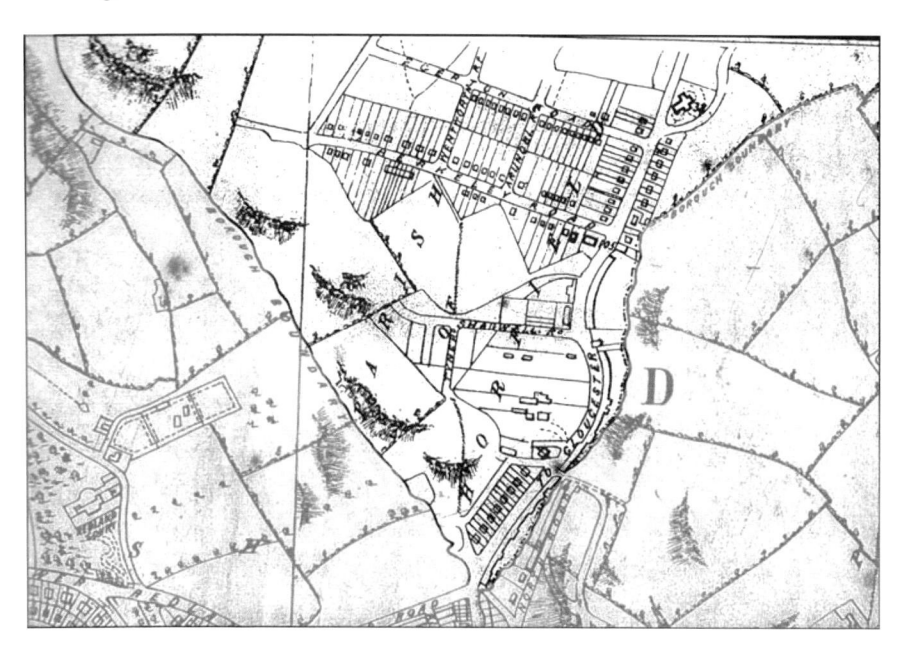

Extract from Lavar's map of Bristol and Suburbs c 1877.

References

1. Wiltshire and Swindon Record Office 1178/642/1.
2. 4d (1.5p) this is approximately equivalent to £1.85 today: http://eh.net/hmit/ppowerbp
3. Bristol Record Office EP/E/11/5
4. Bristol Record Office 40297/E/1

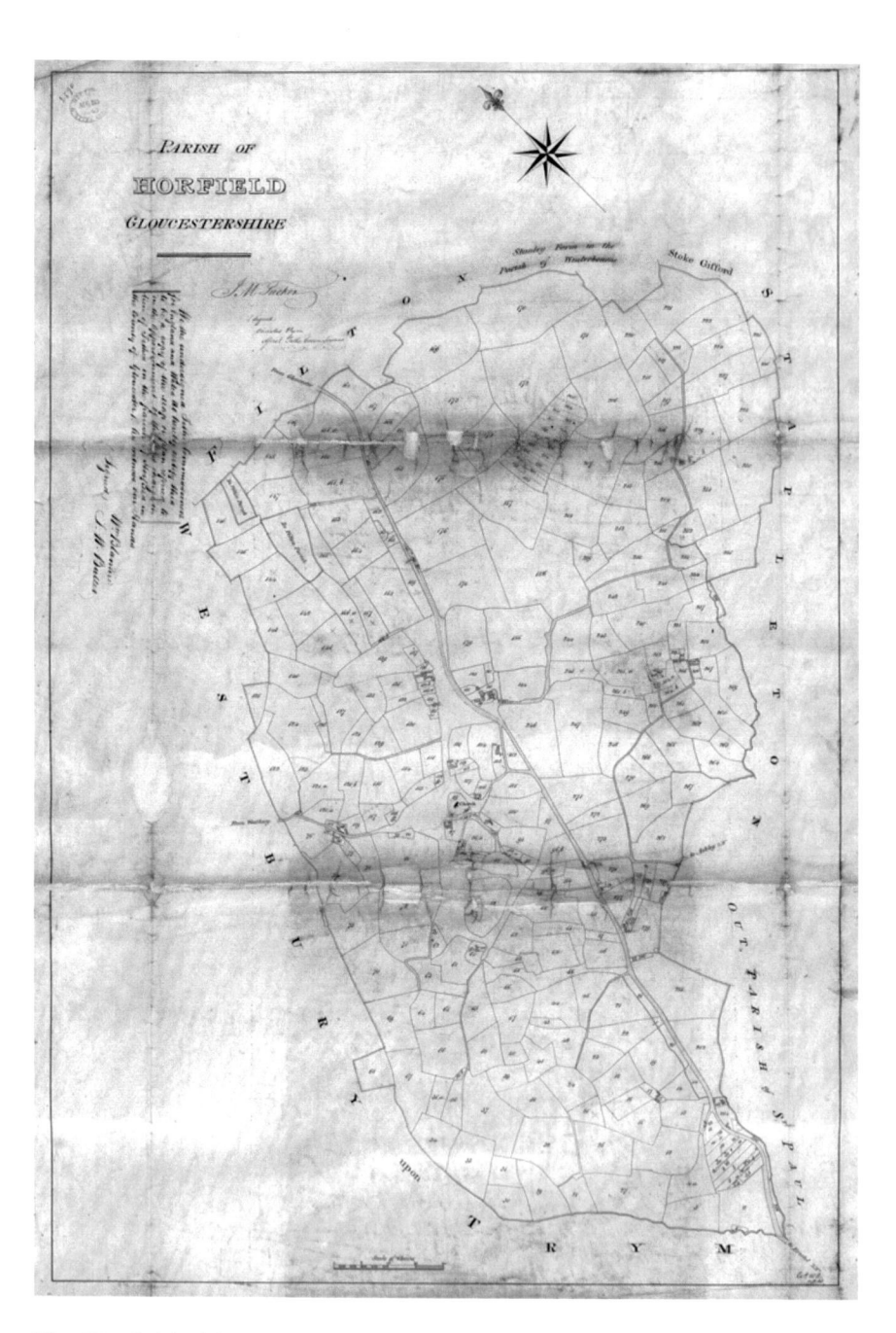

The Horfield Tithe Map – 1841

The Parish of Horfield c 1912-13

Appendix 1   **Horfield Parish Tithe Survey**
[*surveyed 1841, published 1843*]

Apportionment of the Rent Charge in lieu of Tithes in the Parish of Horfield in the County of Gloucester

Whereas an Award of rent charge in lieu of Tithes in the Parish of Horfield in the County of Gloucester was on the twenty ninth day of July in the year One thousand eight hundred and forty one confirmed by the Tithe Commissioners for England and Wales of which Award with the Schedules thereunto annexed the following is a Copy

Know all then by these presents

Whereas I Charles Pym have been duly appointed and sworn an Assistant Tithe Commissioner according to the Provision of the Act for the Commutation of Tithes in England and Wales and have been also duly appointed to ascertain and award the total sums to be paid by way of rent charges instead of the tithes of the Parish of Horfield in the County of Gloucester

And whereas I have held divers meetings near the said Parish touching the matter aforesaid of which meetings due notice was given for the information of Land Owners and Tithe Owners of the Parish

And whereas I have duly considered all the allegations and proofs tendered to me by all parties interested and have myself made all inquiries touching the premised subject which appeared to me to be necessary

And whereas I find that the Lord Bishop of Gloucester and Bristol is Appropriator of the tithes as well Great as small arising from the Lands of the said Parish specified in the third Schedule hereunto annexed and that John Shadwell of the Town and County of Southampton Esquire holds a Lease of the said Appropriate tithes

That the said Lord Bishop is Appropriator of the tithes of Corn and Grain arising from the Lands specified in the fourth Schedule hereunto and that the said John Shadwell holds a Lease of the said Appropriate tithes

That the said Lord Bishop is Appropriator of all the tithes or to the Customary payments in lieu thereof arising from all the Lands specified in the second Schedule hereunto

And that the said John Shadwell holds a lease of the said Appropriate tithes other then [*sic*] the tithes of Hay

And that Anthony Mervin Reeve Storey of Basset Down House in the County of Wilts Esquire, Edward Russell of Montpellier Esquire William Bennett of Clifton and Sarah Gully of Stokes Croft Widow in the City and County of Bristol hold a Lease of the said Appropriate tithes of Hay

That the said Lord Bishop is Appropriator of all the tithes other then tithes of Corn arising from the Lands specified in the fifth Schedule hereunto

And Thomas Lempriere of Saint Heliers in the Island of Jersey Esquire holds a lease of the said Appropriate tithes

I do hereby award the undermentioned Sums to be paid by way of rent charges subject to the provision of the said Act from the first day of October preceding the Confirmation of the Apportionment of the same that is to say

To the said John Shadwell his executors administrators and assigns during the Continuance of his said Lease and after the expiration or other determination thereof then to the Lord Bishop aforesaid and his Successors in the said See the annual sum of One hundred and eighty five pounds in lieu of tithes as well Great as small arising from the Lands specified in the said third Schedule [*Copyholds*]

And the further annual sum of Five pounds and five shillings in lieu of tithes of Corn and Grain arising from the Lands specified in the fourth Schedule [*Lamb's Corn/Grain*]

And the further annual sum of Twenty five shillings in lieu of all tithes other then the tithe of Hay arising from the Lands specified in the said second Schedule [*Great Farm modus*]

To the said Thomas Lempriere his executors administrators and assigns during the Continuance of the said Lease and after the expiration or other determination thereof then to the Lord Bishop aforesaid and his Successors in the said See the annual sum of eight pounds and ten shillings in lieu of all the tithes other than tithes of Corn arising from the Lands specified in the said fifth Schedule [*Lamb's non-Corn/Grain*]

To the said Anthony Mervin Reeve Storey the annual sum of eighteen pounds

To the said Edward Russell the annual sum of twenty five shillings

To the said William Bennett the annual sum of fifty shillings

To the said Sarah Gully the annual sum of five shillings which said several sums shall be paid to the said Anthony Mervin Reeve Storey Edward Russell William Bennett and Sarah Gully respectively and their respective heirs and assigns during the Continuance of their said Lease and after the expiration or other determination thereof then to the Lord Bishop aforesaid and his Successors in the said See instead of the tithes of Hay arising from the Lands specified in the sixth Schedule hereto. [*Great Farm Hay*]

The foregoing several rent charges not only to be in lieu of all tithes payable in kind but also in lieu of all moduses and compositions real and prescriptive and Customary payments payable in respect of all the Lands of the said Parish of Horfield

In witness whereof I the said Charles Pym do hereby affix my hand this twentieth day of July in the year of our Lord One thousand eight hundred and forty one

signed Charles Pym

[*Six schedules then display the above ownership, acreages, and rents in tabular form*]

Now We Young Sturge and John Millard Tucker of the City and County of Bristol Surveyors, having been duly appointed Valuers to apportion the Total Sum Awarded to be paid by way of Rent charge in lieu of Tithes amongst the several Lands of the said Parish of Horfield

Do hereby apportion the Rent charges as follows

Gross Rent charge payable to the Tithe Owners in lieu of Tithes for the Parish of Horfield in the County of Gloucester, Two hundred and twenty two Pounds viz.

To the Appropriator or his Lessee John Shadwell	£191.10s.0d
Thomas Lempriere	£ 8.10s.0d
Anthony Storey	£ 18. 0s.0d
Edward Russell	£ 1. 5s.0d
William Bennett	£ 2.10s.0d
Sarah Gully	£ 0. 5s.0d

Value in Imperial Bushels and Decimal Parts of an Imperial Bushel of Wheat Barley and Oats viz

Wheat 7s.0.25d (210.80119) Barley 3s.11.5d (373.89474) Oats 2s.9d (538.18182)

[*Confirmed by Wm Blamire & TW Buller 26th September 1843, seal 21st November*]

NOTE: In the following apportionment document, information on individual plots was displayed under the following headings: name of occupier, plot number, plot name, state of cultivation, acreage, and rent charge. For reasons of space all the entries in column 4, state of cultivation, have been abbreviated (a=arable, p=pasture, w=wood, pl=plantation, p/o=pasture orchard, and g=garden). Asterisked items refer to further notes at the end.

Two columns were available for entries on rent charge. The first of them was headed 'Payable to the Appropriator or his lessees' and was the one used throughout most of this document. The bishop was the Appropriator but rents went to his lessees. So, for instance rents from copyhold farms went to John Shadwell and rents from the Great Farm to Anthony Storey. Edward

Russell, William Bennett, and Sarah Gulley also collected rents from their small leaseholds. The second rent charge column was headed 'Payable to other lessees'. It was used in the Horfield survey only in the case of an estate known as Lamb's which was effectively a sub-lease from the bishop via John Shadwell to Thomas Lempriere. Occupiers of 3 of those fields also paid a rent charge to John Shadwell.

Leaseholders are shown in upper case letters and so are Copyholders, simply to distinguish them from their sub-tenants. Copyholders were technically responsible for rent charges but in practice payment devolved to sub-tenants.

COPYHOLD ESTATES

DAVID DAVIES

				Area			Rent Payable to the Appropriator or his lessees			Rent Payable to other lessees		
			a	r	p	£	s	d	£	s	d
Himself & William Harford	190	In Huttom Wood*		0	2	5	0	0	5			
	28	Haselton	p	3	0	12	0	14	5			
	38	Gaskins	p									
	39	Further Hinder Moors	p	[8	0	3]*	1	14	0			
	41	Hither Hinder Moors	p	3	1	2	0	14	4			
	54	Rough Leaze	p	4	1	28	1	6	0			
	55	Long Mead & The Rag	p	5	1	28	1	12	0			
	60	House & Homestead		1	0	27	0	6	7			
	61	Allhays	p	4	1	6	1	6	2			
	70	Smillings	p	10	0	36	2	8	0			
	80	Great & Little Hughes	p	9	1	24	2	9	3			
	188	In Huttom Wood		1	0	13	0	0	10			

			a	r	p	£	s	d	£	s	d
William Herniman	12	Broadway	p	8	2	37	2	11	2		
James Ford	79	Cottage & Garden	p	0	2	22	0	5	0		
			Tot	60	1	3	15	8	2		

HENRY HARE Clerk

[*Occupier not identified]	221	Lockleaze	p	11	3	16	1	10	8		
	234	Further Stone Hill	p	1	2	7	0	6	9		
	235	Seven Acres	a	9	0	3	2	11	0		
	236	Part of Seven Acres	p								
	237	Stone Hill	p								
	238	Stone Hills & Home Mead	p	[5	3	8]*	1	12	4		
	239	House & Homestead		0	3	2	0	6	6		
	240	The Barley Ground	p	8	3	24	2	6	8		
	241	Short Mead	a	4	1	9	1	8	4		
	255	Part of Old Orchard & Lane	p	0	3	35	0	5	9		
	269	Great Axtons	p	6	0	15	1	12	0		

			a	r	p	£	s	d	£	s	d
William Smith											
270	Little Axtons	p	3	1	8	0	17	5			
194	In Huttom Wood		0	3	8	0	0	7			
248	Innocks*	p	4	1	24	1	2	9			
250	Part of Long Crate	p	1	1	9	0	7	9			
251a	Remainder of Long Crate	p									
251b	Home Mead	p	[7	0	35]*	2	0	8			
252	Orchard	p/o	1	3	24	0	13	5			
253	House & Homestead		0	3	10	0	6	9			
254a	Part of Old Orchard	p									
254b	Part of Old Orchard	p	[2	0	7]*	0	9	8			
262	Dunghill Close	p	3	2	32	1	0	9			
264	Part of West Close	a	4	2	33	11	17	2			
265	Part of West Close	p	5	1	4	1	8	6			
267	Part of West Close	p	4	1	14	1	2	9			
189	In Huttom Wood		0	3	8	0	0	7			
		Tot	89	3	15	23	8	9			

HENRY RICHARDS Clerk

				a	r	p	£	s	d
Himself	85b	Outbuildings, Yard etc		0	0	38	0	1	4
	86a	Part of Home Mead	p	2	3	0	0	16	10
	86b	Part of Home Mead	p	0	3	7	0	4	10
	192	In Huttom Wood		0	2	32	0	0	6
	195	In Huttom Wood		0	2	32	0	0	6
	200	In Hottom Wood		0	2	25	0	0	6
Joseph Bennett	46	New Leaze	p	3	3	0	1	2	0
	47	Vicarge Mead Paddock	p	1	0	11	0	6	3
Elizabeth Bryant	285	The Paddock	p	1	0	37	0	8	0
Samuel Fry	4a	Broadway	p	4	3	17	1	8	6
	4b	Lane adjoining		0	0	24	0	0	11
	13	Part of Quarry Ground	p	3	2	34	1	2	9
	14	Part of Quarry Ground & Lower Leaze	p	3	1	8	1	0	1
	15	Part of Great Hortley	a	5	0	20	2	3	3
	16	Part of Great Hortley	a	2	2	24	1	1	0

			a	r	p	£	s	d	£	s	d
17	House, Outbuildings Orchard		0	3	1	0	3	7			
18	Middle Hortley	a	4	1	35	1	15	5			
19	Seven Acres	p	6	2	6	1	18	5			
20	Upper Leaze	a	1	0	16	0	9	4			
24	Hither Hortley	a	5	0	14	2	0	2			
92a	House & Garden		0	2	12	0	5	9			
93	Outbuildings, Barton etc		0	2	18	0	6	0			
97	Paddock	p	2	1	31	0	14	2			
98	Home Ground	p	3	2	28	1	1	7			
222	Further Lockleaze	a	6	2	8	1	5	7			
224	Lockleazes	a	6	1	29	1	5	2			
225	Upper Lockleaze	a	1	3	18	0	7	11			
226	Brake in Upper Lockleaze		1	1	12	0	0	8			
227	Hither Locleaze	a	7	1	37	1	9	3			
282	Mill Still Ground*	p	8	0	24	2	8	0			
249	Innocks	p	4	1	24	1	3	0			

48

				a	r	p	£	s	d	£	s	d
John Gray	277	Little Bittons	p	2	2	19	0	16	0			
James Marmont	84	House Yard & Garden		1	0	20	0	8	10			
	85a	Part of Home Mead	p	0	1	19	0	2	2			
Joseph Musty	26	Anders Leaze	p	8	1	30	2	3	6			
	29	Lower Bushy Ground	p	6	2	13	1	10	11			
	30	Part of Upper Ground	p	4	1	22	0	18	7			
	31	Part of Upper Ground	a	2	3	6	0	18	9			
	33	Golden Hill	p	7	1	36	1	7	0			
	36	Golden Hill	p	2	2	19	0	9	11			
Timothy Smith	53	Gaskins	p	2	3	26	0	16	6			
	56	Broadmead	p	3	2	1	0	18	5			
	57	Lower Gaskins	p	4	2	38	1	4	4			
	58	Further Gaskins	a	4	1	20	1	9	5			
	59	Hither Gaskins	p	4	3	28	1	5	5			
	64	Golden Hill	a	2	2	27	0	17	7			
	81	House & Homestead		0	3	14	0	7	6			

49

			a	r	p	£	s	d	£	s	d
82	Home Mead	p	5	2	21	1	13	0			
44	Breery Leaze*	a	5	0	0	1	15	8			
Thomas Vowles											
214	Lockleaze	p	6	0	26	1	4	6			
243	Berry Lane Field	p	3	2	14	0	16	10			
James Weymouth											
220	Webbs Paddock	p	6	3	3	0	19	9			
		Tot	180	2	23	48	15	10			

RICHARD LAMBERT

			a	r	p	£	s	d	£	s	d
43	Gaskins	p	1	0	3	0	4	6			
62	House & Garden		1	0	25	0	5	6			
198	In Huttom Wood		0	2	20	0	0	6			
		Tot	2	3	8	0	10	6			

CATHERINE MARIA ANN HUNT

			a	r	p	£	s	d	£	s	d
Herself											
197	In Huttom Wood		0	2	12	0	0	5			
James Marmont											
101	Churchways	p	3	1	16	0	19	8			
272	The Rudd	p	2	2	19	0	14	4			
John Pope											
21	Great Breakley*	p	7	1	9	2	1	0			
22	Breakly Mead	p	4	3	12	1	5	3			

			a	r	p	£	s	d	£	s	d
	23	Dry Leaze	p	4	0	35	0	18	10		
	45	Horse Leaze	p	4	0	34	1	0	8		
Henry Rumley	108	Part of Home Mead	g	0	1	31	0	4	5		
Reuben Rosling	99	Half Acre	a	0	2	17	0	5	6		
	105	House Stable & Garden		0	0	25	0	3	5		
William Thomas	106	House & Garden		0	2	22	0	3	8		
	107	Home Mead	a	1	1	32	0	13	7		
		Tot		30	1	24	8	10	9		

HENRY EUGENE SHADWELL Esq.

			a	r	p	£	s	d	£	s	d
Himself	191	In Huttom Wood		0	2	39	0	0	6		
	193	In Huttom Wood		0	2	9	0	0	5		
	196	In Huttom Wood		0	2	18	0	0	6		
	199	In Huttom Wood		0	2	19	0	0	6		
	202	In Huttom Wood		0	2	26	0	0	6		
	204	In Huttom Wood		1	0	37	0	0	11		
	205	In Huttom Wood		1	3	35	0	1	5		

				a	r	p	£	s	d	£	s	d
Francis Barnes	103	House Offices & Garden		1	0	18	0	8	9			
	104	Home Mead	p	4	0	27	1	5	6			
--Beakes	111	The Hill	p	2	0	24	0	17	5			
	112	House Stable & Garden		0	1	20	0	4	3			
	113	Home Mead	p	1	2	5	0	8	1			
George Harrison	130	Home Mead	p	6	0	32	1	12	0			
	131	House & Homestead		0	3	24	0	7	2			
	132	The Paddock	p	1	1	9	0	6	9			
	133a	Part of Old Orchard	a	0	1	9	0	1	6			
	136	Rick Barton		0	1	19	0	1	11			
	137	Old Orchard	a	0	3	11	0	6	6			
	138	The Burnt Ground	p	3	0	36	0	15	8			
	139	Dymocks Mead	p	7	2	2	1	16	6			
	145	The Four & Two Acres	a	7	0	6	1	15	9			
	146	Oaky Ground	a	5	2	19	1	7	2			

			a	r	p	£	s	d	£	s	d
James Marmont	34	Golden Hills	p	5	0	4	0	15	0			
	49	Part of Rowlays	P	0	2	33	0	4	3			
	50	The Quab	p	5	0	19	1	10	0			
	67	Golden Hills	p	7	3	32	1	10	7			
	68	Golden Hill	a	4	0	28	1	3	6			
	94	The Common Paddock	p	3	1	16	0	18	1			
	96a	Beech Shord	a	1	2	20	0	8	10			
	100	Churchways	p	5	0	4	1	10	6			
	118	House & Homestead		0	2	23	0	5	6			
	119	Orchard	p/o	1	0	28	0	8	9			
	120a	Home Mead	p	2	0	0	0	11	5			
	120b	Home Mead	p	4	1	0	1	4	0			
	128	Little Hill	p	2	0	26	0	10	3			
	129	Great Hill	p	3	2	37	0	17	8			
	271	Churchways	p	7	3	16	2	3	0			
	273	Mill Leaze	p	6	2	23	1	12	8			

				a	r	p	£	s	d	£	s	d
Elizabeth Matthews	274	House & Garden	p	0	0	34	0	1	1			
John Pope	27	Great Haselton & Cattle Sheds	p	11	2	37	3	3	6			
	32	Great Gout Shord	p	10	3	3	2	8	3			
Peregrine Rosling	35a	Golden Hill	p	2	0	37	0	8	5			
	35b	Golden Hill	p	0	0	39	0	1	0			
	37	Gout Shord	p	10	3	18	2	1	0			
	63	Hither Allhays	p	3	2	12	0	18	9			
	65	Middle Allhays	p	2	3	3	0	13	0			
	66	Further Allhays	a	7	3	16	2	12	3			
	69	Golden Hill	a	7	2	2	2	7	6			
	73	Smillings	a	6	3	24	2	3	8			
	74	Homemead	p	7	3	13	1	19	4			
	75	Barn Close	p	4	0	0	1	1	0			
	76	House & Homestead		0	2	0	0	4	10			
	77	Orchard	p/o	0	2	37	0	5	8			
	78	Wellon Hays	p	3	2	20	1	0	0			

54

			a	r	p	£	s	d	£	s	d
121a	Greening Field	a	5	0	22	1	14	7			
121b	Strip Adjoining		0	0	5	0	0	2			
122	The Ground over the Way	p	9	1	19	1	17	6			
123	Part of Greening Field	a	1	1	3	0	8	0			
125	The Hawes*	a	2	1	5	0	12	10			
126	Long Mead	p	1	2	8	0	6	7			
127	Rowlides	p	6	3	21	1	6	0			
Reuben Rosling											
40	Gaskins	a	1	2	17	0	11	6			
48	Rowlays	p	3	3	15	1	2	7			
217	Lockleaze	p	2	2	25	0	7	7			
218	Lockleaze	a	4	0	20	0	13	10			
219	Lower Lockleaze	p	2	2	13	0	6	8			
223	Lower Lockleaze	p	2	0	33	0	5	10			
230	Seven & Four Acres	p	13	0	0	2	0	6			
231	Nine Acres	p	9	3	38	1	15	0			
Henry Rumley											
109	House & Garden		0	2	27	0	6	3			

				a	r	p	£	s	d	£	s	d
Philip Pincombe	286	The Paddock	p	1	0	0	0	5	4			
William Smith	266	Dowing Paddock	p	3	1	8	0	17	5			
John Taylor	96b	Beech Shord	a	3	0	0	0	19	3			
George Weston	110	Orchard	p/o	2	0	16	0	17	4			
	147	Upper Hare Leaze	p	5	3	16	1	0	7			
	148	Lower Hare Leaze	p	7	1	29	1	4	6			
William Evans	275	Nursery		2	2	37	1	0	7			
	276	House & Nursery		0	2	0	0	3	9			
--Boardman	11	House & Garden		1	0	18	0	5	2			
	10	House & Garden		1	0	1	0	4	9			
Henry Neylor	7	House & Garden		1	1	28	0	6	8			
	8	Houses & Gardens		2	0	26	0	10	1			
	9	Houses & Gardens		1	0	18	0	5	3			
Henry Andrews	6	Houses & Gardens		1	1	15	0	6	4			
--Panes	5a	House & Garden		0	1	0	0	1	2			
	5b	House & Garden		0	2	38	0	3	6			

				a	r	p	£	s	d	£	s	d
Mary Frost	283-4	Houses & Gardens		1	1	27	0	6	8			
			Tot	295	1	36	71	16	8			

JOHN MITCHELL EUGENE TAYLOR SHADWELL

				a	r	p	£	s	d	£	s	d
Himself	201	In Huttom Wood		0	2	12	0	0	5			
James Marmont	117	Home Mead	p	2	1	28	0	14	3			
Reuben Rosling	215	Lockleaze	p	2	3	1	0	10	5			
William Ryall	42	Gaskins	p	5	1	13	1	3	9			
	116	Four Tenements & Gardens		0	3	14	0	7	2			
			Tot	11	3	28	2	16	0			

SIR JOHN SYMTH Bart

				a	r	p	£	s	d	£	s	d
John Bailey	203	In Huttom Wood		0	2	5	0	0	5			
	228	Upper Lockleaze	a	9	1	12	1	16	6			
	229	Lower Lockleaze	a	7	1	20	1	7	8			
	256	House & Homestead		0	2	20	0	6	0			
	257	Orchard	p/o	1	1	21	0	8	11			
	258	Home Mead & Old Fishpond	p	4	1	3	1	5	0			

			a	r	p	£	s	d	£	s	d
259	Great & Little Hills	a	6	1	38	2	14	10			
260	Long Mead	p	5	0	24	1	9	2			
261	Lane Paddock	p	2	2	0	0	14	1			
263	Long Mead Paddock	p	2	1	0	0	11	11			
268	Burlands	a	7	1	33	2	18	10			
		Tot	47	1	16	13	13	4			

LEASEHOLD ESTATES
THOMAS LEMPRIERE Esq.

George Harrison

			a	r	p	£	s	d	£	s	d
133b	Part of Old Orchard	a	0	1	9						
134	Barn Barton etc		0	2	26				0	5	0
135	Home Mead	p	2	2	25				0	18	9

Reuben Rosling

209	Porkers Mead	p	2	3	20				0	13	10
210	Lockleazes	p	7	1	7				1	9	3
211	Further Lockleaze	p	1	0	1				0	5	2
212	Whites Mead	p	6	2	12				1	9	7
213	Whites Mead	p	4	1	20				0	19	8

			a	r	p	£	s	d	£	s	d
232	Upper Well Paddock	p	2	3	21				0	16	6
233	Lower Well	p	2	0	31				0	12	3
242	Berry Lane Field	a	4	3	4	1	10	0	0	5	6
124	North Field	a	10	2	17	3	5	0	0	12	0
150	Horfield Wood	a	2	3	38	0	10	0	0	2	6
		Tot	49	0	31	5	5	0	8	10	0

Peregrine Rosling

George Weston

ANTHONY MERVIN REEVE STOREY Esq

165	Horfield Wood		3	1	25						
169	Finny Mead*	a	16	3	36	1	5	0			
170	Shute Close	a	21	1	24						
171	Shearmore	a	11	1	16						
172	Great Oaken Bush Leaze	a	18	2	25						
173	Little Oaken Bush Leaze	a	13	3	35						
174	Little Elm Bush Leaze	p	7	3	23						

John Hember Jnr

		a	r	p	£	s	d	£	s	d
175	Great Elm Bush Leaze	p	10	3	1	1	8	0			
176	East Bartholomew Leaze	p	14	3	25	1	17	0			
178	West Bartholomew Leaze	p	12	2	1	1	11	0			
179	Rose Mead & Grove	p	7	3	19	1	4	0			
180	Great Orchard	p/o	1	3	26	0	4	0			
181	House Offices Homestead		2	2	38						
184	Orchard	p/o	4	2	20	0	11	0			
185	Home Mead	p	12	1	26	1	17	0			
186	Wooden Bridge Ground	p	21	0	3	2	14	0			
187	Bushy Innocks	p	13	2	27	1	14	0			
206	East New Leaze	a	14	1	6						
207	Middle New Leaze	a	12	2	4						
208	West New Leaze	a	9	3	5						
216	Quab Mead	p	5	1	19	0	14	0			
246	Upper Innocks	p	9	1	37	1	14	0			

			a	r	p	£	s	d	£	s	d
247	Lower Innocks	p	15	2	29	2	12	0			
		Tot	263	0	30	18	0	0			

The next four are lessees under Anthony Mervin Reeve Storey

EDWARD RUSSELL

			a	r	p	£	s	d	£	s	d
114	[East Hill]	p	3	2	27	0	11	0			
115	[West Hill]	p	4	2	21	0	14	0			
280	House etc[Part of Horse Hill]		0	0	35						
279	Houses [Bynland]		11	0	15						
281	Houses [Horse Hill]		13	3	2						
		Tot	33	1	20	1	5	0			

WILLIAM BENNETT

			a	r	p	£	s	d	£	s	d
2	East Conygre	p	8	1	9	1	10	0			
3	West Conygre	p	6	0	26	1	0	0			
		Tot	14	1	35	2	10	0			

SARAH GULLEY

			a	r	p	£	s	d	£	s	d
102	Part of Upper Innocks	p	1	2	30	0	5	0			

WILLIAM SCUDDER

			a	r	p	£	s	d	£	s	d
William Vowles	149	Hare Leaze	a	2	3	35					

ABRAHAM MAGGS

				a	r	p						
	1	Conygre Dell Cottsge & Garden	a	0	1	8						
			Tot	53	3	8						

Tithe Free Lands (The Demesne)
JOHN SHADWELL Esq

				a	r	p						
William Bennett	166	Horfield Wood	p	4	0	11						
	167	Wood leaze	p	4	2	14						
John Gardner	278	Strip of Waste	pl	0	0	14						
William Harford	71	Little Mill Furlong	a	4	1	27						
	72	Great Mill Furlong	p	8	1	8						
George Harrison	140	The Five Acres	a	5	1	28						
	141	Home Mead	a	7	3	19						
	142	Old Pool Leaze	a	6	3	32						

62

			a	r	p	£	s	d	£	s	d
143	Five Acre Field	p	5	0	35						
144	Stubby Leaze	p	7	3	32						
153	Further Great Breach	p	5	3	38						
154	Middle Great Breach	p	6	1	13						
155	Further Breach Mead	a	3	3	9						
156a	Old Orchard	p	5	3	8						
156b	Lane		0	0	29						
157	Hither Breach	a	3	3	13						
158	Great Breach	p	9	1	16						
159	Hither Cow Leaze	p	3	2	16						
161	The Brake	w	0	1	28						
162	Further Cow Leaze	p	1	2	27						
83	The Paddock	p	2	0	14						

James Marmont

				a	r	p	£	s	d	£	s	d
Henry Richards	88	Plantation adjacent Churchyard		0	0	18						
	89	Churchyard		1	1	0						
	90	Plantation		0	0	33						
Reuben Rosling	244	Berry Lane Field	p	5	3	35						
	245	Berry Lane Field	p	2	3	8						
Eleonor Sanders	183	Cottage & Garden		0	0	15						
James Thomas	91	Cottage & Garden		0	0	24						
	92b	Part of Old Lane & Garden		0	0	20						
George Thomas	177c	Cottage Garden etc		0	0	18						
Joseph Tilly	51	Vicarage Mead	p	3	0	23						
	52	The Quab	p	3	3	38						
John Pope	25	Hortley	p	2	1	1						
John Vickery	160	Further Cow Leaze	a	0	2	11						
	177b	Cottage etc		0	0	3						

				a	r	p	£	s	d	£	s	d
George Weston	151a	Horfield Wood	a	8	0	18						
	151b	Horfield Wood	a	9	0	14						
	152	Lane		0	2	8						
	163	Horfield Wood	a	8	0	37						
	164	Strip adj. Horfield Wood	g	0	0	25						
Mary Weston	168	Hight[on?] Wood	a	4	0	25						
Isaac Young	177a	Cottage		0	0	21						
			Tot	148	3	26						
Commissioners of Bristol Turnpike roads												
Thomas Book	95	Cottage & Garden		0	0	7						
Henry Richards (Clerk) Glebe												
Himself	87	House Offices Pleasure Gardens		1	0	20						
Commons				33	3	22						
Roads				19	1	24						
			Tot	53	1	6						

Notes

1. Occupiers.* No occupier name was given for one of Henry Hare's two farms. The usual method of recording occupiers suggests that it was James Ford but other factors, including Ford's known occupation as a florist, indicate that the farm was actually awaiting a new tenant. Similarly, information seems to have been unavailable about the first names of three other occupiers, recorded as Beakes, Boardman, and Panes.

2. Field Names.* To avoid confusion, field names are recorded exactly as they appeared in the tithe survey even though some are questionable. A minor clerical error (21 Great Breakley/ 22 Breakly Mead) is therefore left uncorrected and so are those cases where field names recorded in 1841 differed from all known earlier versions.
   Huttom Wood (188-205). In manorial records, the wood was always called 'Hutton'.
   Breery Leaze (44). In manorial records, the field appeared twice as 'Briary Leaze'.
   Finny Mead (169). In a lease of 1532, the field was called Trynnysmeade and variant spellings in subsequent leases always began with the letters 'Tr'.

The published script of the tithe survey seems to have led to decoding errors even amongst contemporary readers. A printed list of field names at enfranchisement (Schedule 2, House of Commons, 1852) contained the following:
   Innocks (248) as 'Junocks'; Mill Still Ground (282) as 'Mile Stile Ground';
   Breery Leaze (44 above) as 'Berry Leaze'; The Hawes (125) as 'The Hawse';
   and Burlands (268) as 'Binlands'.
However, one clerical error (above) was resolved by printing 'Breakly' for both fields.

3. Acreages.* On four occasions, the tithe survey gave a composite acreage for two or more copyhold fields. Schedule 2 (1852) supplied separate acreages (but not separate rent charges) for each field as follows:

David Davies	a)	38	Gaskins	5 0 13
		39	Further Hinder Moors	2 3 30
				(tot. 8 0 3)